Kind

D1147001

Axel Scheffler is the award-winning illustrator of some of the best-loved children's books in the world. Born in Germany, he lives in the UK and especially likes drawing red squirrels.

Sir Quentin Blake has drawn ever since he can remember. He was the first ever Children's Laureate, and his much-loved books include *Mister Magnolia* and his collaborations with Roald Dahl.

Beatrice Alemagna has won many awards for her work including the Italian Andersen Prize for Illustrator of the Year. Born in Italy, she decided, aged eight, to be a writer and painter.

Serge Bloch is an internationally renowned French illustrator. He's a storyteller, an entertainer, a smuggler of ideas and lover of jokes, who builds his stories brick by brick, like a house.

Steve Antony is the prize-winning creator of *Please Mr Panda*. He is passionate about literacy and inclusiveness, and his work is influenced by his red-green colour blindness.

Melissa Castrillón finds lots of illustration ideas in nature. She especially loves drawing plants and flowers, and is inspired by the Cambridgeshire countryside where she lives.

David Barrow is an illustrator, story-creator and general scribble-monger. He loves spinning a story from a simple idea, and finds that long walks help him work out the plot.

Benjamin Chaud is the much-loved French author and illustrator of over sixty books. He goes sketching in a café every morning, and always tries to include cats and dogs in his books.

Rotraut Susanne Berner is one of Germany's most acclaimed illustrators and has won many awards. She has illustrated over 150 books and almost eight hundred book covers.

Marianna Coppo lives in Rome and spends all day drawing (when she's not sleeping or eating bruschetta). She loves children's books, mayonnaise and unexpected travel.

Kitty Crowther is part-English, part-Swedish and lives in Belgium. Winner of the prestigious Astrid Lindgren Award, her work is influenced by the wonderful books she had as a child.

Thank you to all the kind illustrators who donated their work for free in aid of the Three Peas charity.

Pippa Curnick was a book designer before becoming an illustrator. She's an avid reader, walker and biscuit-lover, and is also a whizz at puppet- and model-making.

Ingrid Godon loved drawing more than any other school subject. She writes her own books, too, and especially likes drawing poetic, sensitive pictures of people and places.

Gerda Dendooven is a celebrated Belgian illustrator, author, and occasional actor. She uses pencils, ink and collage to make her humorous, expressionistic pictures.

Susanne Göhlich is a much-loved German illustrator. Her many books feature lots of people; every animal you can imagine – and ten very adventurous ghosts!

Michael Foreman is one of the UK's most acclaimed illustrators. He has illustrated over 300 books, and has travelled around the world from the Arctic to the South Pacific to research them.

Chris Haughton grew up in Dublin but has lived all round the world, from San Francisco to Kathmandu. His quirky, brilliantly colourful books have won him international acclaim.

Lucia Gaggiotti likes to express joy, happiness and fun in her pictures. She says that drawing children's books lets her step inside the page and live in that world.

Nicola Kinnear is an illustrator, storyteller and maker of beautiful things (she's especially good at crochet). She loves to bring magic, nature and folklore into her books.

First published in the UK in 2019 by Alison Green Books
An imprint of Scholastic Children's Books
Euston House, 24 Eversholt Street
London NW1 1DB
A division of Scholastic Ltd
www.scholastic.co.uk
London – New York – Toronto – Sydney – Auckland
Mexico City – New Delhi – Hong Kong
Designed by Zoë Tucker

This paperback edition published in 2020

Text by Alison Green © 2019 Scholastic Children's Books

Illustrations copyright © 2019 Beatrice Alemagna, Steve Antony, David Barrow, Rotraut Susanne Berner,
Sir Quentin Blake, Serge Bloch, Melissa Castrillón, Benjamin Chaud, Marianna Coppo, Kitty Crowther, Pippa Curnick,
Gerda Dendooven, Michael Foreman, Lucia Gaggiotti, Ingrid Godon, Susanne Göhlich, Chris Haughton, Nicola Kinnear,
Ole Könnecke, Anke Kuhl, Sarah McIntyre, Dorothée de Monfreid, Lydia Monks, Jörg Mühle, Thomas Müller, Barbara
Nascimbeni, Guy Parker-Rees, Moni Port, David Roberts, Axel Scheffler, Nick Sharratt, Birgitta Sif, Helen Stephens,
Lizzy Stewart, Britta Teckentrup, Philip Waechter, Ken Wilson-Max, Cindy Wume

Three Peas logo copyright © 2018 Three Peas
Three Peas photo © 2019 Ulla Wilde
Reproduced by permission

ISBN: 978 0702301 74 2

All rights reserved.
Printed in Malaysia

3 5 7 9 10 8 6 4

The moral rights of the author and illustrators have been asserted.
Papers used by Scholastic Children's Books are made from
wood grown in sustainable forests.

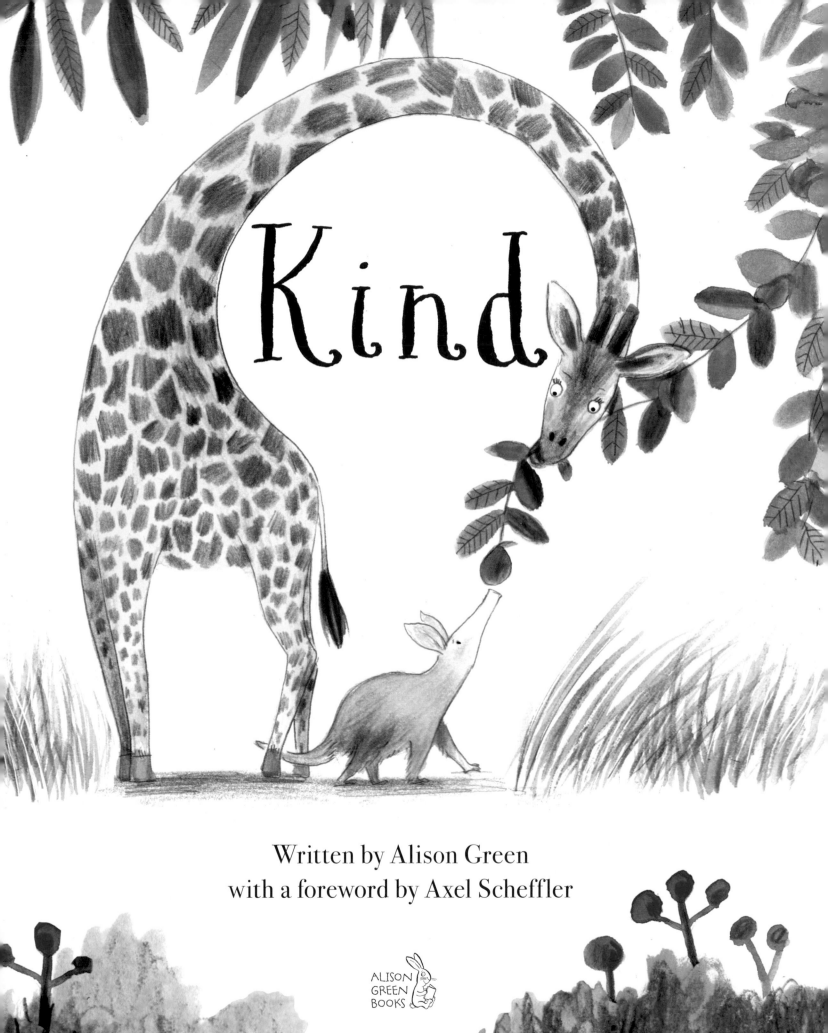

Kind

Written by Alison Green
with a foreword by Axel Scheffler

ALISON
GREEN
BOOKS

What can you do to be kind today?

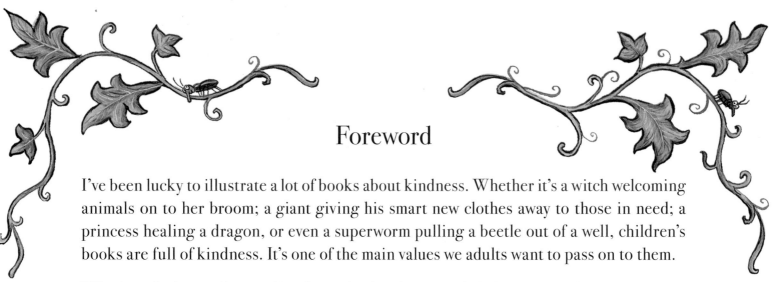

Foreword

I've been lucky to illustrate a lot of books about kindness. Whether it's a witch welcoming animals on to her broom; a giant giving his smart new clothes away to those in need; a princess healing a dragon, or even a superworm pulling a beetle out of a well, children's books are full of kindness. It's one of the main values we adults want to pass on to them.

Whether it's the small acts of kindness that brighten our daily lives, or the bigger questions of how we help those in real need, we know that a kinder world is a better world.

But sometimes it feels as if we're just too busy to stop and give a hand to those who need it. Sometimes we feel helpless, as if nothing we do will make enough of a difference. It's good to remind ourselves that even the smallest acts of kindness really can make an impact.

The world seems full of division at the moment, but I believe passionately that it's only by being kind, generous, open and compassionate that we'll make a peaceful, prosperous world for the next generation.

I have been patron of the Three Peas charity for over two years, and have seen how much of a difference small acts of kindness can make to those who are in desperate need. Three Peas is a charity that has helped make a difference in the lives of many refugees in the most desperate circumstances, and I'm proud to be supporting their vital work.

I hope that both children and adults will enjoy exploring this book. It's full of amazing illustrations by many of the world's top illustrators, who have all donated their work for free. The images they've created are joyful, funny, moving and inspiring. They feature monkeys, elephants, lions, cats, dogs, worms – and even people! And they show us many simple ways in which we can all help to make the world a better place.

Axel Scheffler, 2019

Imagine a world where everyone is kind.
How can we make that come true?

Here's a good place to start –

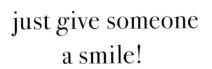
just give someone
a smile!

There are lots
of good ways
to be kind.

We can listen to people,
especially when they're sad.

We can give them a hug
if they're feeling lonely.

If someone's frightened or worried,
we can offer to hold their hand.

If they're in trouble, we can see if we can help.

Can you tell someone
a story to cheer
them up?

It's good to listen to
their stories, too.

And let's make sure
no one's left out when
we're playing a game

and that everyone
is cared for.

Have you ever made
a Kindness Jar?

Every time you do something kind,
put a marble or a button into it.
I bet you'll soon fill it up!

What else can you do to be kind today?
Here are some good ideas.

Can you help carry a bag?

Or pick up things people have dropped?

Or let someone else
go in front of you?

It's really kind to be patient
– especially when you don't feel like it!

Animals need lots of kindness, too.

What do you do best?

We're all good at different things,
so let's give everyone the chance to shine.

Sometimes extra kindness is needed,
such as when you meet someone
who's new where you live.
Can you be a good friend
and help them feel
at home?

What's their favourite game?

Is it a quiet one?

Or a really noisy one?

If they're trying to learn our language,
perhaps you can tell them new words?

home

good morning

hello

laugh

school
help
play
peace

family
love

my friend

welcom

happiness
breakfast
kind

How about learning some words from
their language, too? Look at all these
different ways of saying, "Hello!"

Sometimes people have lived through
very hard times. They've had to leave their
homes and their countries because of danger.

They are brave and amazing and
have extraordinary stories to tell.

How can you welcome them?
Can you share your toys
with them?

Or draw pictures
together?

Sometimes people say
we don't have enough to share,
and there's no room for anyone
more. But maybe you can say,
"There's plenty of room!
Come on in!"

After all, if you don't let people in, you'll never know what you're missing. There might be a wonderful new friend just outside the door.

Everyone is valuable,
and we all have gifts to share.

Let's be curious about the world
and all the people in it.

It's fun to see what we do the same,

and what we do differently.

Everyone can be kind,

even if they're really small
or a bit shy.

It feels nice to be kind.
And it's a good idea, too.
Because if everyone is kind . . .

. . . we'll make a better world.

Three Peas – Help make a difference!

This book is helping to raise money for the charity Three Peas,
which gives vital practical help to people who have had to flee their homes.

It takes a lot of courage to leave your home, to leave everything behind, and to travel to another country, but that's what many people around the world are forced to do.

There might be a war where they live and their homes are no longer safe. Or they might come from countries where they're not allowed to live the way they want to, or say what they want to, or practise their religion. They feel they have no choice but to leave and find a safer place to live.

They have to make long, difficult, dangerous journeys. When they finally arrive in their new countries, they have to apply for permission to stay – a process that can take years. During that time it's hard for families to find work or even somewhere to live.

That's where organisations like Three Peas can lend a hand. They may help people find a home, and can provide basic supplies of clothes, food and all sorts of essential items from shampoo and toothbrushes to books and prams.

After so much upheaval, families long for a bit of normality. They want to cook food together and celebrate their feast days. They want to learn the local language. They want to work and support their families, and they want their children to have a good education.

Many people have skills that they used in their old lives, which they're keen to use again. They may be doctors, teachers, lawyers or artists. Some of the people that Three Peas have met have volunteered as maths teachers and translators. Others have gone on to make a living as hairdressers, restaurant owners, jewellery designers and even sculptors.

Three Peas help run a centre where people can take language classes, receive advice and make friends. They even helped three little girls find an after-school dance class, which really helped them settle into their new country.

As people learn the language of their new country, and their children go to school, they can start to make safe, new, happy lives for themselves.

photo © Ulla Wilde

Three Peas was started by a group of friends from six different countries.
They are a small organisation, but have achieved an amazing amount. As they say:
"Imagine if every single one of us did something small to help? Together we could make a big difference!"
You can find out more about Three Peas here: www.threepeas.org.uk

THREE PEAS
HELP MAKE A DIFFERENCE

Thank you to all the kind illustrators who donated their work for free in aid of the Three Peas charity.

Lydia Monks is the award-winning illustrator of the *What the Ladybird Heard* series by Julia Donaldson. She has a poodle called Chadwick who likes to distract her while she's working.

Ole Könnecke has received many awards for his illustration. Born in Germany, he grew up in Sweden, and his style of drawing owes a lot to the comics he loved as a child.

Jörg Mühle is a German illustrator who creates irresistible pictures of rabbits, penguins, bears and many more. He is quite tall and has an awful lot of dots on his name.

Anke Kuhl likes to draw pictures with a dark sense of humour (she even has a couple of little skeleton models on her desk.) She also likes to relax by cooking or playing the piano.

Thomas Müller illustrates stunning theatre posters as well as beautiful children's books. He lives in Leipzig and enjoys walking in the woods and collecting classic cars.

Sarah McIntyre has illustrated books featuring everything from Dinosaur Firefighters and Jampires to Cakes in Space. She loves dressing up and owns lots of dramatic hats.

Barbara Nascimbeni is an Italian-born illustrator who creates richly coloured pictures. She lives in Germany and France and also enjoys gardening and playing the accordion.

Dorothée de Monfreid created a host of entertaining dogs for her books *A Day with Dogs* and *SHHH! I'm Sleeping*. Based in Paris, she also loves to write and draw comics.

Guy Parker-Rees is the acclaimed illustrator of *Giraffes Can't Dance* and *Dylan*. He has drawn and doodled all his life, loves cake, and has his best ideas when sitting under a tree.

 **Moni Port** is an award-winning German illustrator. She worked as a bookseller before studying illustration, and is married to fellow artist Philip Waechter.

 **Lizzy Stewart** is the creator of the award-winning book, *There's a Tiger in the Garden*. When not drawing, Lizzy enjoys swimming and walking a small dog named Peanut.

 **David Roberts** started out as a hat-maker and then switched to illustration. His favourite things to draw are people laughing and wearing fabulous clothes.

 **Britta Teckentrup** writes and illustrates books in both English and German. Her rich, colourful artwork uses a mix of handmade and digital techniques and has won many prizes.

 **Nick Sharratt** created pictures for magazines and Easter egg wrappers before becoming one of the UK's favourite book illustrators. He has won many prizes and even has a gold Blue Peter badge.

 **Philip Waechter** creates stories that are inspired by his own life. He keeps a visual diary, drawing a small picture every day and is married to fellow artist, Moni Port.

 **Birgitta Sif** has won fans around the world with her exquisite, heartfelt illustrations. Born in Iceland, she grew up in Scandinavia and America and now lives in England.

 **Ken Wilson-Max** has illustrated over fifty children's books. He was born and raised in Zimbabwe, and his work celebrates the fact that people are more similar than they are different.

 **Helen Stephens** loves drawing from life, and does her best drawings in the rain! She has illustrated over fifty books, and is best known for the bestselling *How to Hide a Lion* series.

 **Cindy Wume** is a Taiwanese illustrator based in Taipei. Her drawing is inspired by a mixture of real life and imagination, and she loves reading and collecting picture books.